St. James
Catholic School
Montague, Michigan

GEARING DOWN

Author

Sam Moses

Photography

Heinz Kluetmeier

William M. Delaney
Dave Friedman
Susan Mann
Lee Stanley

St. James
Catholic School
Montague, Michigan

Published by **Advanced Learning Concepts, Inc.**
Milwaukee, Wisconsin

A Product of **Advanced Learning Concepts, Inc.**
and Follett Publishing Company
A Division of Follett Corporation
Chicago, Illinois

Contents

1 A Growing Sport   6

2 From Bicycle To Bike   12

3 The New Rage   20

4 A Tricky Game   30

5 An Event For Everybody   34

6 Hot, Sandy...And Risky   42

7 Life In The Pros   50

8 Tight Race   56

Pre-Reading Aids   65

Discussion Questions   73

Related Activities   74

1
A Growing Sport

Millions of kids have grown up with such athletes as Hank Aaron, Billie Jean King, or Joe Namath as their heroes. Kids train hard to be able to do the same things their heroes can. But how many kids eat their spinach so they will grow up to be like Marty Tripes? Probably not very many, because he isn't very well-known.

There's a reason why Marty Tripes isn't a big name, like Aaron, King, or Namath. Marty Tripes is a motorcycle racer, and in the United States, motorcycle sports are just beginning to become popular. They don't get into the news the way other sports do. Except in places where motorcycling is big, like California, most people don't know who the motorcycling stars are.

In Europe, however, motorcycles have been popular for a long time, both for transportation and for competition.

Motorcycles are cheaper to buy than cars and they are also cheaper to run. A one-cylinder cycle may get up to sixty miles per gallon. That's about two or three times as much as the average small car. Add to this the high price of gasoline and the fact that many European city streets are just too narrow for cars, and it's easy to see why motor-

cycles have been accepted as a good way to get around.

Motorcycle races in Europe are more of a happening than in the United States. During road races, European fans line the streets of their towns to watch their favorites zoom by. In the United States, motorcycle sports are usually held far away from the cities. There are no races in the United States which attract three hundred thousand people and wind through scenic areas, like the Belgian Grand Prix or the race on the Isle of Man.

The motorcyclist has always been somewhat of a hero in Europe, too. When Joel Robert won the 250cc motocross title, for example, he was named Outstanding Belgian Athlete of the Year.

Americans still think of cyclists as "Hell's Angels." Many parents don't want their children to grow up to be motorcyclists. They feel that cyclists are bad. It's something to think about. Is a person who owns a "chopper" always bad? Are motorcycle athletes really different from people in other sports?

Some people must think so. When companies are asked if they would like a motorcycle star to advertise their products, they often are afraid. They're nervous about what the people who buy their products will think. Many times a racer will be brought in to meet with someone from a company. The motorcyclist often ends up looking very much like any other athlete.

Safety is another touchy issue. People often feel that the chance for injury is higher on motorcycles than in cars. That problem has been solved somewhat by laws which require cyclists to wear helmets. And the American Motorcycle Association makes a good point: They note that the National Safety Council says that sixty to seventy percent of street accidents between motorcycles and cars are caused by drivers of the cars.

The people involved in motorcycle sports are very safety-minded. "How To" books on racing warn beginners about "wheelies." They say wheelies not only lose time for a racer, but can result in broken bones. Cyclists are also advised to dress right for each motorcycle sport. Footwear is a good example. In dirt track racing, riders drag a foot on the ground as they turn corners. So they wear boots with steel toes. High, laced boots are useful for desert racing. They are better than steel-toed boots because they're easier to unlace and remove if a toe is broken. Beginning riders in observed trials usually wear boots that cover the ankles. The boots help prevent pegs on the bike from cutting into the ankles.

Helmets are a familiar part of a cyclist's gear. But how many people know that many riders wear kidney belts? A kidney belt is useful during falls. It helps the rider from getting scrambled inside during jarring rides.

Deaths in professional racing vary from year to year. In 1973, nine racers died. Only two died in 1974. When thinking about these figures, consider how many people were racing. In 1974, there were about seven hundred events under the direction of the American Motorcycle Association. About one hundred riders were in each event. In other words, there were seventy thousand chances for a death. Two occurred. Two too many. But not as bad as nine.

2
From Bicycle To Bike

Whatever the dangers, motorcycle sports are starting to become really big news in the United States. Motorcycle racing has been around for a long time. Americans have been racing motorcycles almost as long as they've been playing baseball.

Back in the mid-1800s, when baseball was invented, the motorcycle was dreamed up by Gottleib Daimler, a German inventor. Daimler put a benzine-fueled, one-cylinder engine on a bicycle. He would heat the fuel in a glass tube, then push the cycle to turn over the cylinder. Once the thing was going, Daimler would jump on it and be off. Considering its beginnings, it's not surprising that the motorcycle is often called a "bike" today.

Naturally, as soon as the first motorcycle rolled out of Daimler's garage, people wanted to find out who could ride the fastest. In those days, most people thought anyone who rode — much less raced — such a contraption had to be fearless. So riders had nicknames like Fearless, Cannonball, Crazy Horse, and Mile-a-Minute.

Riders were called board trackers because the tracks they raced on were made of wooden boards. The wood wasn't polished like a basketball court. It was rough two-by-

fours with cracks and holes, like an old picnic table.

At one of the board tracks, kids sneaked into the races by crawling underneath the board surface. The holes in the boards were so big the kids could stick their heads up through them for a close-up view. A rider could be flying along at top speed and see a kid's head suddenly pop up out of the track.

The board track motorcycles had no throttles. The riders used a switch on the handlebars to control their speed. In the "off" position, the engine would die. In the "on" position, the engine was at full throttle. There was nothing in between. The machines could go over one hundred miles an hour. And they had no brakes.

For protection the riders wore only high, lace-up boots, baggy leather pants, and leather flying caps. Crashes were frequent. Many riders were thrown off their cycles and ended up with splinters in the seats of their pants.

And even back in the old days, motorcycling had its Evel Knievel-like showmen. In 1913, an American named Don Johns raced his Cyclone motorcycle around a mile oval track against a big Lincoln car and a low-flying airplane. The motorcycle won and Johns collected one thousand dollars.

Board track racing reached its peak about 1915. Gradually the board tracks became overgrown with weeds. Dirt track racing became more and more popular until World War II, when there was very little motorcycle racing.

County and state fairs were usually the scene of the best dirt track races, especially in the Midwest in late summer. There is still a national championship dirt track race at the Indianapolis fairgrounds. Dirt tracking was, and still is, the real nitty-gritty of American motorcycle racing.

Motorcycle racing of all kinds has come a long way since World War II. After Europe got back on its feet after the war, English, German, and Italian motorcycles were brought into the United States in increasing numbers. With them came many new ideas in motorcycle racing. Compared to the solid but simple American models, the European bikes were fancy. They could do things the American machines couldn't, such as racing on twisting pavement.

Today, professional American riders have the best equipment available. And they are the highest-paid of all motorcycle racers in the world. The best racers can make over one hundred thousand dollars a year, a top salary for any athlete.

Many different types of competitions — professional and amateur — are available to the motorcycle enthusiast. There is everything from hill climbing (where riders try to climb steep slopes at the base of mountains) to indoor short track (where they race around ovals about the size of a basketball court) to drag racing. Cyclists also race on paved surfaces like the famous Daytona Speedway, where the cycles go nearly 180 miles an hour. They race on half-mile or one-mile dirt ovals. They race in the desert.

Some competitors take part in events which are not actually races. In the observed trials, for instance, riders try to pass through a short course without touching a foot to the ground. In enduros, riders try to maintain certain speeds, in order to arrive at checkpoints at an exact time.

Beginning in the early 1970s, motocross became the most popular type of motorcycle sport in America. Motocross had been popular in Europe since the end of World War II. But it didn't spread to the United States until 1966. That year, the great Swedish world champion, Torsten Hallman, came to the U.S. for nine exhibition races. He proved

that the European professional motocross racers were far more skilled than the Americans. Until then, Americans knew little of the fancy European riding techniques. And they were unaware of the Europeans' greater attention to physical conditioning. The Americans were eager to learn. And they learned fast.

3
The New Rage

Motocross is tougher on the body than any other sport but soccer.

A certain amount of strength is required to be a good motocross racer. But most important are balance, reflexes, and conditioning. The best motocross racers are more like swimmers than like weight lifters or football players.

A professional motocross consists of two forty-five-minute heat races, called motos. Racing full speed for forty-five minutes on a bouncing motocross machine is like running wind sprints in football gear for forty-five minutes. Or wrestling fifteen periods without a break. To make things a little easier, there is usually an hour between the two motos for the riders to rest and for the mechanics to make any needed repairs to the machines.

Motocross can be dangerous. But it isn't as risky as dirt tracking and road racing, where the speeds are twice as high. In motocross, there is the risk of broken collarbones and twisted ankles, and occasionally a rider may suffer a broken arm or leg.

To cut down on injuries, a motocross racer wears padded leather pants and gloves, stiff boots, a baseball catcher's shin guards and chest protector, shatterproof goggles, and a helmet with a mouth guard.

Usually, motocross races are held outdoors. The motocross tracks are about a mile long. They include steep dirt hills, jarring ruts, gooey mudholes, and frightening jumps. Then there are "whoop-de-doos," which are a series of small jumps. Riding over whoop-de-doos is like sitting on the handle of a jackhammer. Some of the biggest jumps send the riders and their machines flying six feet into the air at sixty miles an hour.

Sometimes, motocross tracks are built indoors, in stadiums like the Los Angeles Coliseum or the Houston Astrodome. And while these are man-made race courses, the jumps and whoop-de-doos are just as hard on the rider.

Motocross cycles are lightweight trail bikes which have been souped-up. All the "extras," such as lights and horns, are removed. The engines, which have been improved and changed for motocross racing, are very powerful.

Motocross is one of the fastest-growing sports in the United States. Americans compete in it successfully, but they can't claim that they invented it. Although motocross began in England in the 1920s, the French gave it its name. They put together "moto" (for motorcycle) and "cross" (for cross-country race). Motocross, as it exists today, is, in part, the result of the lack of entertainment available following World War II. Someone in France got the idea that motocross would be a cheap and exciting form of entertainment. The riders were thought of as entertainers rather than athletes. Motocross wasn't a sport, but a circus.

Today motocross is considered both good entertainment and good sport. At an amateur motocross, a rider can expect to see several hundred other racers and anywhere from a handful to a few thousand people watching. The riders who do well might win a trophy. But even if they don't,

they know they have made full use of their athletic ability, courage, and mechanical skill (if they work on their own motorcycles).

At a professional motocross, the riders are usually divided into two groups: Novice and Expert. The Novices are not nearly as competitive with each other as the Experts, so their machines don't need to be so powerful. A small bike used for riding in the woods is often fast enough to race in the Novice class.

Professional motocross racers are in the "big league" of racing. There are three professional classes, based on engine size: 500cc (cubic centimeter) for the biggest and fastest bikes, the 250cc class, and the 125cc class.

Motocross racers who compete professionally travel around the country as many as forty weekends a year. Most of them drive in vans with their bikes. But some riders, who are paid by motorcycle companies, fly from race to race. Mechanics carry the bikes for that factory's team in a big truck equipped with expensive tools and spare parts.

All of the large manufacturers — such as Honda, Yamaha, Kawasaki, Suzuki, Husqvarna, Bultaco, Maico, and CZ — have racing teams. The teams have at least two, and sometimes as many as six riders. The companies back the teams because it's good publicity for them when their motorcycles win. The riders are called factory riders. They are the cream of the crop. There aren't many factory riders. But their numbers are growing as the sport grows.

The companies pay their teams' salaries and expenses. Often they pay a bonus for winning. For example, Jim Weinert was paid a twenty-thousand-dollar bonus by the Kawasaki factory when he won the 500cc National Championship. That was in addition to his prize money.

Many of the professional motocross racers in the U.S. are young. The 1974 250cc national champion, Gary Jones, was twenty-two — and that was his third 250cc championship in a row. The 1974 national champion in the 125cc class was Marty Smith, a seventeen-year-old high school student.

Marty Smith became a champion in only three years. He began racing when he was fourteen on an old 125cc Yamaha that he rode mostly on trails in the woods. When his parents gave him permission to race, he took his little Yamaha to a motocross. He finished fifth against other riders with similar bikes. He kept at it. Three years later he was a paid factory rider for the Honda company.

Of course Marty Smith had great talent. But he also had drive. Without that drive he never would have discovered the talent.

There are others like Marty. In 1974, the runner-up in the 500cc class was seventeen-year-old Tony DiStefano. Brad Lackey was the 1972 500cc national champion at the age of nineteen. In 1974, he was a Husqvarna factory rider, racing in Europe in the summer and in the United States in the fall.

All of the young champions began racing when they were in junior or senior high school. And they all began the same way: entering their own bikes at local motocross races.

The most amazing young rider is Marty Tripes. In 1972, he won the Superbowl of Motocross in the Los Angeles Coliseum, beating the best riders in the world. That week he had just turned sixteen. That's the youngest a racer can be in the American Motorcycle Association. It was his first race as a pro.

4
A Tricky Game

If you think the only way to go on a motorcycle is as fast as possible, be surprised.
One motorcycle sport that's growing very
fast is observed field trials, where riders
travel just a little faster than a crawl.

An observed trials event is not a race. Speed
is more of a problem than a help.

The event usually includes two laps of a
loop which contains up to twenty sections.
Since there are many cycles covering each
section, the sections tend to get torn up. A
section is usually not the same by the time a
rider gets to it a second time.

A section is tricky enough the *first* time a
rider gets to it. Sections are marked by lines
of lime, stakes, string or tape strung from
rocks, trees, and bushes. Obstacles within a
section include sand, rocks, hills, holes full
of water, and narrow areas which are difficult to steer through.

The object of this sport is to pass through a
section without making a mistake. If the
event is run according to American Motorcycle Association rules, a rider starts with a
score of zero. Each time the rider touches a
foot to the ground (called a "dab"), points
are added. The first and second dabs usually
add one point each. Any dabs after that
mean three points each. A rider who comes

to a complete stop gets five points added to the score. Points are also added for other errors, like dropping the cycle or going out-of-bounds. Completing a section without a mistake is called a "clean." The idea is to get as few points as possible.

There is one famous section that is part of the Scottish Six Days Observed Trials. This section is called the "pipeline." It climbs up the face of a steep, rocky mountain. The pipeline is long and narrow. And because it rains almost every day in Scotland in June, when the event is held, the smooth sides of the rocks are as slippery as ice. Even the greatest trials riders in the world think it is a true test of skill to clean the pipeline.

Observed trials has a bright future largely because it demands so little of the outdoors. It only requires a lightweight motorcycle that isn't much louder than a family Ford. And the riding area doesn't have to be much larger than a two-car garage.

It is motorcycling's answer to golf, in that the riders compete one at a time. And since the sections are small, the people watching can gather together in a group. As in golf, the group is silent when riders approach a difficult section so as not to disturb them. If the rider cleans the section, the group breaks into applause, much the way people who follow golf do after a golfer sinks a long putt.

5
An Event For Everybody

For every serious motorcycle racer there are at least a couple dozen racers who compete just for fun. They range from children to people past retirement age. You can find them bouncing around the countryside on any weekend of the year.

These riders like enduros because an enduro is not actually a race. Riding ability is, of course, very important. But the ability to ride fast is not everything. An enduro is a test of wits and strategy.

An average enduro is about one hundred miles long. The course is rough and uneven, but not difficult. The course is marked by arrows and ribbons. Along the trail are six or eight places where the riders must check in.

At the start of the event, a rider is given a time card with average speeds on it. The rider must keep up those averages. The rider's goal is to arrive at the checkpoints (which are hidden) exactly on time. A rider who arrives late loses points. And a rider who arrives early loses twice as many. So riding too fast is worse than riding too slow.

Often there are hundreds of entries for an enduro. Because the trails are narrow, it is impossible to start all the riders at once. So they start one minute apart, in groups of four. This can be hard to take for the serious

enduro rider, who may be carrying a stop-watch and mechanical speed calculator. A beginner without even a speedometer on the motorcycle can follow the rider with the special equipment and, with a little luck, can sometimes come out ahead.

Keeping a steady speed in an enduro sounds easy, and it would be easy enough if there weren't other riders involved. What happens, though, is that traffic jams develop at difficult parts of the course, like a swamp or a steep hill. The enduro rider may be forced to thread his way through the traffic jam by walking his bike through all the mud and traffic. Then the rider has to speed up to maintain the average speed. It gives the enduro all of the excitement of an expressway at rush hour.

Another hassle is mechanical failure. Riders try to prepare themselves by carrying spares of parts which are often lost or broken, like cables and shift levers. More stops for repairs mean more catch-up effort for the rider.

Each enduro has its special problems. Two of the biggest national enduros are the four-hundred-mile Jack Pine in Michigan and the five-hundred-mile Greenhorn in southern California. They are so different that not many riders can do well in both.

In the Jack Pine, the problems are steep slimy hills, muddy forest trails, and sometimes even river crossings. One year the trails were so muddy that hundreds of bikes were backed up at the trouble spots.

The Greenhorn is considered the most punishing of all enduros. It is a sandy two-day affair, held in early summer in California's Mojave Desert. Because the speed averages are usually high in the Greenhorn, the pace is sometimes frantic. It's as close to being a race as an enduro can be. Just to finish the Greenhorn is something to be proud of.

And then there is the International Six Days Trials, the ISDT. ISDT riding requires every kind of talent a rider can have.

There is no prize money in ISDT. Riders compete for gold medals. The ISDT is governed by the Federation Internationale Motorcycliste in Switzerland. It is held in a different country each year.

About three hundred riders from many countries enter the ISDT each year. That's why the ISDT is recognized as the Olympics of motorcycle competition.

There are two-day qualifying events throughout the United States to determine which American riders will compete.

Usually about one-fifth of the riders who compete win gold medals. To win a gold medal, the rider must stick to the established average speed for the six days. There are about a dozen daily checkpoints. At the end of each day, there is a special timed section — usually a motocross race. That race serves as a tie-breaker for those riders who have kept to the average speed. To keep the gold medal, a rider must finish within seventy percent of the fastest rider's time in each class.

At the end of the special test, the riders must park their machines. They can't touch them until ten minutes before starting time the next morning.

Riders cannot replace any major parts of their motorcycles at any time. They must carry all their tools with them. No one may touch either the riders or the bikes.

The event lasts for one thousand miles over rough and sometimes impossible ground. No wonder it is such an achievement to earn an ISDT gold medal.

Czechoslovakia is the team to beat in ISDT competition. The Czechs take the ISDT very seriously. Riders train almost year-around for the competition. The Czechoslovakian

government supports the team members for taking part in the ISDT.

By September, when the ISDT is held, the Czechs are in better shape than any other team. Their motorcycles are tuned down to the tiniest detail, and their organization is military-like. This preparation and skill shows. They win.

The Italian ISDT in 1974 was one of the toughest ever, because the speed average was very high. But six Americans won gold medals. One was twenty-four-year-old Billy Uhl. The Italian ISDT was Uhl's sixth, and it was his fourth gold medal. In the 1969 ISDT held in Germany, he became, at age nineteen, the youngest rider ever to win a gold medal.

6
Hot, Sandy...And Risky

Many enduros in the western part of the United States are held in the desert. But a lot of people who like to ride in the desert find enduros too slow. They like riding as fast as they can. For them, racing in the desert has a special appeal. Most of them live in southern California. Because of the climate, the interest in motorcycles there is high. The weekend playground for off-road motorcyclists is the Mojave Desert, the heart of desert racing in the United States.

Desert racing is a test of courage. It requires the most attention, and it is probably the most dangerous kind of racing. Desert racers ride their bikes at full speed — sixty, seventy, sometimes as much as ninety miles an hour. The surface is unknown. They must count on instinct. Relaxing for just one second could spell disaster. At seventy miles an hour, even the tiniest hole could pitch the bike end-over-end, and the rider could fly over the handlebars. Desert racers spend three to four hours riding in the baking sun, in temperatures ranging from ninety to one hundred thirty degrees. They must cross thirty-mile stretches of rocks or whoop-de-doos.

They must be on the lookout for sharp cactus plants. There is always the threat of un-

seen holes, which hide in the desert floor. Often desert racers have to make the last-second choice: either slam on the brakes or open the throttle wide.

Their muscles ache. Their eyes grow red from the dust and tired from the strain of always looking ahead. But they must never be worn down by fatigue. An error in judgment could mean being stranded in the desert for hours. Or it could mean an injury.

The start of a desert race is one of the most spectacular sights in racing.

The largest motorcycle race in the world, the Barstow-to-Las Vegas desert race, has such a start. Shortly after sunrise, more than 2,000 motorcycles form a line side by side. When the banner drops, they all start their engines and take off together for Las Vegas, 175 miles across the desert. First rider there wins.

Only a handful of the desert races pay any prize money. Most have trophies and pins for riders who finish a race. An off-road rider who wants to win money must compete in events such as the Baja 1000. The Baja starts in Ensenada, Mexico, and runs down the length of the Baja Peninsula to the little fishing village of La Paz.

In 1962, a team of riders made the first Baja run in sixty hours. When they came back with their story, other riders set out to beat them. Soon the run became a full-scale race, with trucks, jeeps, and dune buggies, as well as motorcycles. The winning motorcycle now always finishes the run in under twenty hours. In the 1974 Baja 500 — a shortened version of the Baja 1000 — a 400cc Husqvarna ridden by the team of Mitch Mayes and A. C. Bakken won overall. They beat the expensive four-wheeled racers.

The most astonishing tale of Baja must be that of the young Watkins brothers, Don and Ed. They rode their 70cc Honda minibike in the 1973 Baja 1000. They were still making

payment on the bike. The machine had a top speed of only forty-five miles an hour. They had no pit crew along the way to help. And Don got lost for eight hours on the first night. But they still reached La Paz. It took them over two days and they didn't win anything. But they were the first team ever to finish the trip on a three-hundred-dollar minibike.

And even auto racer Parnelli Jones did not finish that year in his thirty-thousand-dollar Bronco racer.

7
Life In The Pros

The most important and profitable motorcycle racing is done on the national circuit. It is here that the racers compete for the coveted "plate." This is the license plate that has the big black "1" on it. For a professional motorcycle racer, the greatest honor is to be called "Number One."

The national championship season runs from February to October and has about twenty races.

There are five different types of racing on the circuit: road racing, mile, half mile, short track, and Tourist Trophy.

In the United States, road racing is not done on roads. The races take place on tracks which are also used for auto racing, such as the Daytona International Speedway.

In road racing, riders crouch behind sleek moldings that wrap around the front and sides of their bikes. Their chests are pressed to the gas tanks to cut down on wind resistance.

At tracks like Daytona, they reach speeds of over 180 miles an hour. In the turns, they downshift and brake to 40 or 50 miles an hour. The best riders lean over so far they drag their knees on the pavement and rub holes in their clothes. In many ways, road

racing is like a high-speed ballet.

The other four types of races are held on dirt tracks. The mile, half mile, and short track races are on ovals of different lengths. A Tourist Trophy race uses only part of an oval, with a few tight turns and a jump inside.

In the mile, racers hurtle their stripped-down 750cc bikes along the straights at nearly 130 miles an hour. In the turns, they pitch the bikes over so far on their sides that the engine cases drag in the dirt. Mile bikes have a disc brake on the rear wheel that is not often used. Riders slow down for the turns by sliding the bikes sideways. And this move *begins* at 130 miles an hour!

They slide through the turns in groups at ninety miles an hour, with their left legs extended to balance the bikes and their steel-toed shoes dragging on the track. They jostle each other, bumping wheels and riding over each other's toes. Some riders bump others toward the wall to make room to pass. But this is accepted as part of the game. And it is rare for anyone to cry "foul."

An entire season of that kind of riding can be tough. Every racer on the circuit has had a share of broken bones. Some of them have had so many they can't remember them all. In 1974, eight of the top ten riders of 1973 had to miss at least one race because of an injury. It's not an easy way to make a living.

The circuit can be a grind, especially during the summer when most races are held. Most of the riders leave home in July with a van full of racing bikes and tires and tools. They don't return until September. They race three and four nights a week at small tracks to pick up pocket money as they wait for the big national race each Sunday. In one season they can rack up over one hundred thousand miles.

In the 1950s and early 1960s, the average

age of the riders was older than today's average age. When the motorcycle boom hit the United States in the early 1960s, a new crop of kids grew up on bikes. By the late 1960s, there were dozens of talented rookies. Many of them became factory riders. On the track, they took chances the veterans never would. Motorcycle racing took on the personality it has today because of the factory riders.

Kenny Roberts is a good example of the natural motorcycle racer. He is five feet six inches tall, bowed legs and all, and weighs 135 pounds. In 1972, his first year as an Expert, he finished fourth in the national championship. In 1973, he was Number One, and repeated this in 1974. At age twenty-two he was on top of the motorcycle racing world.

He has won at least once at each of the five types of racing, a distinction held by only one other rider — the great Dick Mann. But it took Dick seventeen years to win all five; Roberts needed less than three years.

For two years Kenny has ruled the American national circuit. He has traveled to Europe to race against the best in the world. In Holland, in his first world championship road race, he was leading until he fell off his bike. But he got up and still finished third. In Italy, he shocked the fourteen-time world champion, Giacomo Agostini, by leading the race until his rear tire blew because he was cornering so hard.

By the end of his third year of professional racing, most people agreed that Kenny Roberts was the best motorcycle racer ever. His ability to go faster on a motorcycle than anyone alive earned him nearly two hundred thousand dollars that year.

8
Tight Race

Racing on the national circuit is fiercely competitive. In 1973, for example, the first ten national races were all won by different riders.

The one-mile dirt track at the Santa Clara County Fairgrounds in San Jose, California, seems to have the hardest-fought races in the United States.

In 1958, for example, the lead in the twenty-five-lap race changed hands fifty-five times. But after that race, the San Jose mile event was not held for fourteen years. In 1972, it was added to the national circuit again.

That year, a young rider named Jim Rice passed Kenny Roberts on the last turn to win by less than a wheel length. The amazing thing was that Rice, in cutting the turns so closely, had bumped his shoulder against the rail halfway through the race. He broke his collarbone.

The 1973 race was also a thriller. With only one lap to go, there were six riders within inches of each other. Down the back straight they weaved, each trying to outmaneuver and outsmart the others. At the finish line, Gene Romero nipped his teammate Gary Scott by inches. All six riders were so close they could have been covered by a blanket.

With that kind of history, the 1974 San Jose mile was expected to be an exciting race. And it was. Kenny Roberts, the 1973 national champion, and Gary Scott, the runner-up in two national championships in a row, went at it in both their races. In their qualifying heat, they passed each other again and again for all of the ten laps, with Kenny edging Gary at the end. But that was only a warm-up for the main event.

Twenty tense riders revved their engines as they waited for the green flag to drop. When it did, they roared away from the starting line, crowding each other for position in the first turn. Gary opened up a big lead on the first lap, while Kenny hit an oil slick in Turn One and fell back to fifth position. But then he went to work.

By lap six he was in second place, pushing Gary. For the final nineteen laps they raced like they were chained together, as they played leapfrog on the back straight and cat and mouse in the turn. Neither rider could break away or hold the lead for more than a lap, so it became a race of stategy at 120 miles an hour. Gary would back off the throttle on the back straight, so Kenny would have to pass him. Then Kenny would weave down the front straight, trying to shake Gary out of his slipstream.

As they came out of Turn Two on the last lap, Gary led. As they set up for Turn Three, by sliding sideways, Kenny waited just a fraction of a second. They slid around turns Three and Four, side by side.

There was nothing left now but a two-hundred-yard drag race to the checkered flag. Gary edged ahead. Kenny was on the inside against the rail — on the "groove," where the rubber from the racers' tires builds up a narrow, hard-packed path that gives the rear wheel more traction. Kenny "got a bite" and pulled alongside Gary with just one hundred yards to go. His good drive

out of the last turn carried him past Gary just feet before the finish line. For the second year in a row, Gary had been beaten by inches after being passed in the last turn.

After the race, Kenny said that when he realized he couldn't pull away, he planned his move for the last turn. "It's really satisfying to make a plan like that and then execute it successfully."

Pre-Reading Aids

1
A Growing Sport

Purpose for Reading

Why are motorcycle racers not well-known in the United States?

Is what we think about cyclists and motorcycling fair?

The answers to these questions are in Chapter 1.

Important Vocabulary

The following words may be of help as you read this chapter:

competition (com pe ti tion; kom pə tish′ən), *n.*
the effort to get something wanted by others

The *competition* between the two friends has always been strong—both want to be the best.

happening (hap pen ing; hap′ə ning), *n.*
a special event, an event which often has not been planned

The concert turned into a *happening* as more and more people dropped in and joined in the singing.

scenic (sce nic; sē′nik), *adj.*
describing natural surroundings

She had a *scenic* view from her living room window.

issue (is sue; ish′ü), *n.*
a problem or point to be discussed

Janice wanted to bring up the *issue* of quitting school with her parents before making a decision.

advised (ad vised; ad vīzd′), *v.*
warned, given a suggestion

The weather reporter *advised* motorists to drive carefully because of icy streets.

consider (con sid er; kən sid′ər), *v.*
to think about carefully

The jury was asked to *consider* the evidence before reaching a verdict of guilty or innocent.

Pre-Reading Aids

2
From Bicycle to Bike

Purpose for Reading

How have motorcycles and motorcycle racing changed over the years?

You'll learn the answers as you read Chapter 2.

Important Vocabulary

throttles (throt tles; throt′əlz), *n.*
engine valves which control the flow of fuel

The *throttles* were wide open as the train speeded up.

frequent (fre quent; frē′kwənt), *adj.*
happening often

Sharon made *frequent* trips to see her friend.

gradually (grad u al ly; graj′ü ə lē), *adv.*
little by little

The room was *gradually* filled with people.

nitty-gritty (nit ty grit ty; nit′ē grit′ē), *n.*
the basic part of something

After lunch they got down to the *nitty-gritty* of the problem.

increasing (in creas ing; in krē′sing), *adj.*
becoming greater in number

The *increasing* variety of new cars can be confusing.

pavement (pave ment; pāv′mənt), *n.*
the top layer, or surface, of a street of track

Studded snow tires quickly tore up the *pavement*.

amateur (am a teur; am′ə chür), *adj.*
doing something for pleasure, not for money

Only *amateur* racers can be in the Soap Box Derby.

enthusiast (en thu si ast; en thü′zē ast), *n.*
a person who has strong feelings for something

Don was a sports car *enthusiast*.

Pre-Reading Aids

3
The New Rage

Purpose for Reading

What is motocross?

Why is it one of the toughest sports in the world?

Important Vocabulary

reflexes (re flex es; rē′fleks əz), *n.*
the power to act quickly, without having to think about it

If you're going to drive, you should have good *reflexes.*

occasionally (oc ca sion al ly; ə kā′zhə nə lē), *adv.*
now and then, once in a while

Occasionally, even the best friends fight with each other.

injuries (in jur ies; in′jər ēz), *n.*
damages to the body

The driver of the car received minor *injuries* when she hit a road sign.

jackhammer (jack ham mer; jak′ham ər), *n.*
a drill, using air under pressure to break up rocks or concrete

The sound of the *jackhammer* outside the window gave Ray a headache.

competitive (com pet i tive; kəm pet′ə tiv), *adj.*
able and willing to make the effort required to get something wanted by others

Highly *competitive* companies often try to drive each other out of business.

publicity (pub lic i ty; pub lis′ə tē), *n.*
information designed to attract people's interest

The movie received a great deal of *publicity* before it was released.

talent (tal ent; tal′ənt), *n.*
a special ability

His job was so dull that he did not think he would ever be able to put his *talent* to good use.

Pre-Reading Aids

4
A Tricky Game

Purpose for Reading

Can you imagine a motorcycle sport where you travel little faster than a crawl?

You'll learn about one in Chapter 4.

Important Vocabulary

Here are some words which may prove helpful as you read:

observed (ob served; əb zėrvd′), *adj.*
carefully watched

After his heart attack, Mr. Bramson was a closely *observed* patient in the intensive care ward of the hospital.

obstacles (ob sta cles; ob′stə kəlz), *n.*
things standing in the way

The boat managed to dock safely, avoiding all the underwater *obstacles* in its way.

demands (de mands; di mandz′), *v.*
requires, asks for something

If he *demands* a refund, the store will give him back his money or allow him to take an exchange.

applause (ap plause; ə plôz′), *n.*
clapping hands or shouting to show approval

After the meeting, the *applause* for the speaker lasted for three minutes.

Pre-Reading Aids

5
An Event For Everybody

Purpose for Reading

Why is the enduro so popular?

What is the Olympics of motorcycle racing—the ISDT?

The answers are in this chapter.

Important Vocabulary

These words may be of help as you read Chapter 5:

strategy (strat e gy; strat′ə jē), *n.*
careful planning

With the *strategy* she had worked out, Susan was sure she could win the chess game.

average (av er age; av′rij), *adj.*
estimated or figured out based on arithmetical mean

The *average* price of food has increased sharply in the last ten years.

maintain (main tain; mān tān′), *v.*
to keep up, carry on

Mrs. Richards found it hard to *maintain* her home after her husband died.

frantic (fran tic; fran′tik), *adj.*
very excited, wild with fear or worry

Eric was *frantic* when he couldn't find his brother.

recognized (rec og nized; rek′əg nīzd), *v.*
accepted or granted

Swimming is *recognized* as one of the best kinds of exercise.

qualifying (qual i fy ing; kwol′ə fī ing), *adj.*
successfully passing a test of some type, gaining the right to compete in an event

In the *qualifying* heat, the runner was tripped.

Pre-Reading Aids

6
Hot, Sandy . . . And Risky

Purpose for Reading

Why would anyone want to race across an unknown desert for three to four hours in temperatures above ninety degrees?

You'll learn the answer as you read Chapter 6.

Important Vocabulary

These words may be helpful to you as you read:

appeal (ap peal; ə pēl′), *n.*
a thing of interest, something of attraction

Traveling around the country after high school had a great *appeal* for Valerie.

instinct (in stinct; in′stingkt), *n.*
a natural feeling, knowledge or power

His eyes were covered, so he had to depend on his *instinct* to get out of the room.

disaster (dis as ter; də zas′tər), *n.*
an event that causes much suffering or loss

The tornado was thought to be the greatest *disaster* ever to hit that county.

fatigue (fa tigue; fə tēg′), *n.*
tired feeling caused by too much work or lack of sleep

Her *fatigue* showed in the dark circles under her eyes.

spectacular (spec tac u lar; spek tak′yə lər), *adj.*
showy, striking

The fireworks were a *spectacular* sight, lighting up the whole sky.

version (ver sion; ver′zhən), *n.*
a special account or description

The child's *version* of what had happened was very different from anyone else's.

Pre-Reading Aids

7
Life in the Pros

Purpose for Reading What is it like on the national circuit?
How old are the cyclists who race to become Number One?

The answers are in this chapter.

Important Vocabulary You may find the following words helpful as you read this chapter:

profitable (prof it a ble; prof′ə tə bəl), *adj.*
bringing in money, giving a gain or benefit

Learning to repair small motors and appliances might be a *profitable* skill.

coveted (cov et ed; kuv′ə təd), *adj.*
wished for, eagerly desired

Winning the *coveted* award made Ginny feel very proud of herself.

ballet (bal let; bal′ā), *n.*
a storytelling dance, accompanied by music written especially for it

Tickets for the *ballet* are usually quite expensive.

extended (ex tend ed; ek sten′dəd), *adj.*
stretched out

The *extended* rubber band finally snapped because of the strain of stretching it around the package.

personality (per son al i ty; pėr sə nal′ə tē), *n.*
the quality that makes one person different from another

Lenny's choice in clothing gives more than a hint of his *personality*.

distinction (dis tinc tion; dis tingk′shən), *n.*
a sign of honor, excellence

Maggie's *distinction* is that she is the first female sportswriter for the newspaper.

Pre-Reading Aids

8
Tight Race

Purpose for Reading

What makes the difference when two cyclists race neck and neck all the way?

You'll learn the answer as you read this chapter.

Important Vocabulary

You may find the following words helpful as you read this chapter:

outmaneuver (out ma neu ver; out mə nü′vər), *v.*
to outdo, to get the better of

Rob ends up with the kitchen chores because he cannot *outmaneuver* his two older brothers.

traction (trac tion; trak′shən), *n.*
friction of a wheel on the road or track

Snow tires give added *traction* in deep snow.

satisfying (sat is fy ing; sat′is fī ing), *v.*
fulfilling a person's wants and hopes

It was *satisfying* to know his work was finished and Isaac would have the next three days to do as he pleased.

Discussion Questions

Chapter 1

What would you say to a friend's parents to convince them to allow your friend to buy a motorcycle?

Chapter 2

What are the two *major differences* between motorcycling today and in earlier years?

Chapter 3

If a member of your class asked you whether motocross racing would be a good sport to try, what would you say?

Chapter 4

Attack or defend the idea that observed field trials is not a sport at all.

Chapter 5

How would you persuade a friend to take part in an enduro event with you?

Chapter 6

What is the appeal of desert racing?

Chapter 7

Would you accept or reject the argument that the demands of the national circuit schedule—not greater skills—have made national circuit racing a sport for the very young.

Chapter 8

Imagine an interview with Gary Scott just after the San Jose Mile in 1974. What might Scott say?

How would he explain being narrowly beaten for the second year in a row?

Related Activities

1. Create a motorcycling game based on an event of interest to you. Teach one or more of your classmates to play.

2. Visit your library or a newsstand. Make a list of the motorcycle magazines which seem the most interesting. Include subscription cost and a brief description of each magazine. Post the list in your classroom.

3. Write to one or both of the following addresses and request free information about motorcycling: Motorcycle Industry Council, 1001 Connecticut Avenue, Washington, D.C. 20036; American Motorcycle Association, P.O. Box 141, Westerville, Ohio 43081. Make this information available to your class.

4. Put together a dictionary of motorcycle terms that would be useful to someone who is unfamiliar with the sport.

5. Ride a motorcycle—as the driver or passenger. How is motorcycling different from other types of transportation? What is its appeal? Record your feelings on paper, on tape, or in some other way and share them with your class.

6. Visit your school or public library. Find some resources about motorcycling. List each of these, together with a brief description. Post your list in your classroom.

7. Write to the Rusty Bradley Memorial Scholarship Fund, c/o Savings Department, First National Bank of Boston, P.O. Box 2016, Boston, Massachusetts. Ask for information about the fund. Make this information available to your class.

8. Contact an organization concerned about ecology (for example, the Audubon Society). Ask their help in determining how motorcycles may be harmful to the environment. Make a list of common sense rules for motorcyclists that will help protect the environment. Explain your list to your classmates.

9. Write to the U.S. Geological Survey, Washington, D.C. 20242, and ask for their free booklet, "Topographic Maps." Use this booklet and sample maps (available at a library or from many stationery and office supply stores) to explain to your class how to read topographic maps. Find out how the maps can be useful to motorcyclists and report to your class.

10. Invite the owner of a motorcycle shop to visit your class. Ask the owner to speak on matters of interest to you and your friends. Be sure to write a letter of thanks.

11. Make and display a poster advertising a motorcycle race.

12. Write to the American Motorcycle Association (the address is given in Activity 3) and ask for information on the following:
    the championship point system
    the schedule of major championship events for this year
    history of the American Motorcycle Association
    Make this information available to your classmates.

13. Collect pictures from magazines and newspapers that capture the feeling of motorcycling. Display your pictures.

14. Organize a motorcycling corner in your classroom. Display the results of these and other activities there.

15. Draw a diagram of a motorcycle. Label and display it.

16. Write to the American Motorcycle Association and ask for a copy of the rule book for the type of motorcycle racing that most interests you. Make the book available to your class.

17. Make a diagram or model of an enduro which you design. Explain your creation to your class.

18. Write to the American Motorcycle Association and ask for the name and address of the regional field representative who lives closest to you. Contact the representative and ask for one or more of the following:
    names and addresses of pro racers in your area
    dates and locations of races in your area
    Make your information available to your class.

19. Attend a motorcycle race or watch one on television. Report your impressions to your classmates.

20. Watch the newspapers and some national sports magazines for articles on motorcycling. Clip and post them in your class.

Reading and Curriculum Editor	Peter Sanders, PhD. Wayne State University
Associate Reading Consultants	John Clark, M.A. Cincinnati Public Schools Cincinnati, Ohio Edward Daughtrey, M.S. Norfolk City Schools Norfolk, Virginia
Story Editor	Patrick Reardon
Associate Editor	Deborah Gardner
Coordinator of Learner Verification	Peter Sanders, PhD.
Related Activities and Vocabulary Sections	Peter Sanders, PhD.
Photography Editor	Eric Bartelt
Graphic Design	Interface Design Group, Inc.

Color Process	American Color Systems
Lithography	A. Hoen & Co.
Binding	Lake Book Bindery

St. James
Catholic School
Montague, Michigan

Lee Stanley's photography courtesy of *Cycle Guide* magazine

Manufactured in the United States of America to Class A specifications of The Book Manufacturers' Institute

2 3 4 5 6 7 8 9 0   80 79 78 77 76